This book belongs to:

....

Copyright © BPA Publishing Ltd 2020

Author: Pip Reid
Illustrator: Thomas Barnett
Creative Director: Curtis Reid

www.biblepathwayadventures.com

Thank you for supporting Bible Pathway Adventures®. Our adventure series helps parents teach their children more about the Bible in a fun creative way. Designed for the whole family, Bible Pathway Adventures' mission is to help bring discipleship back into homes around the world. The search for truth is more fun than tradition!

The moral rights of author and illustrator have been asserted, this book is copyright.

ISBN: 978-0-473-37659-8

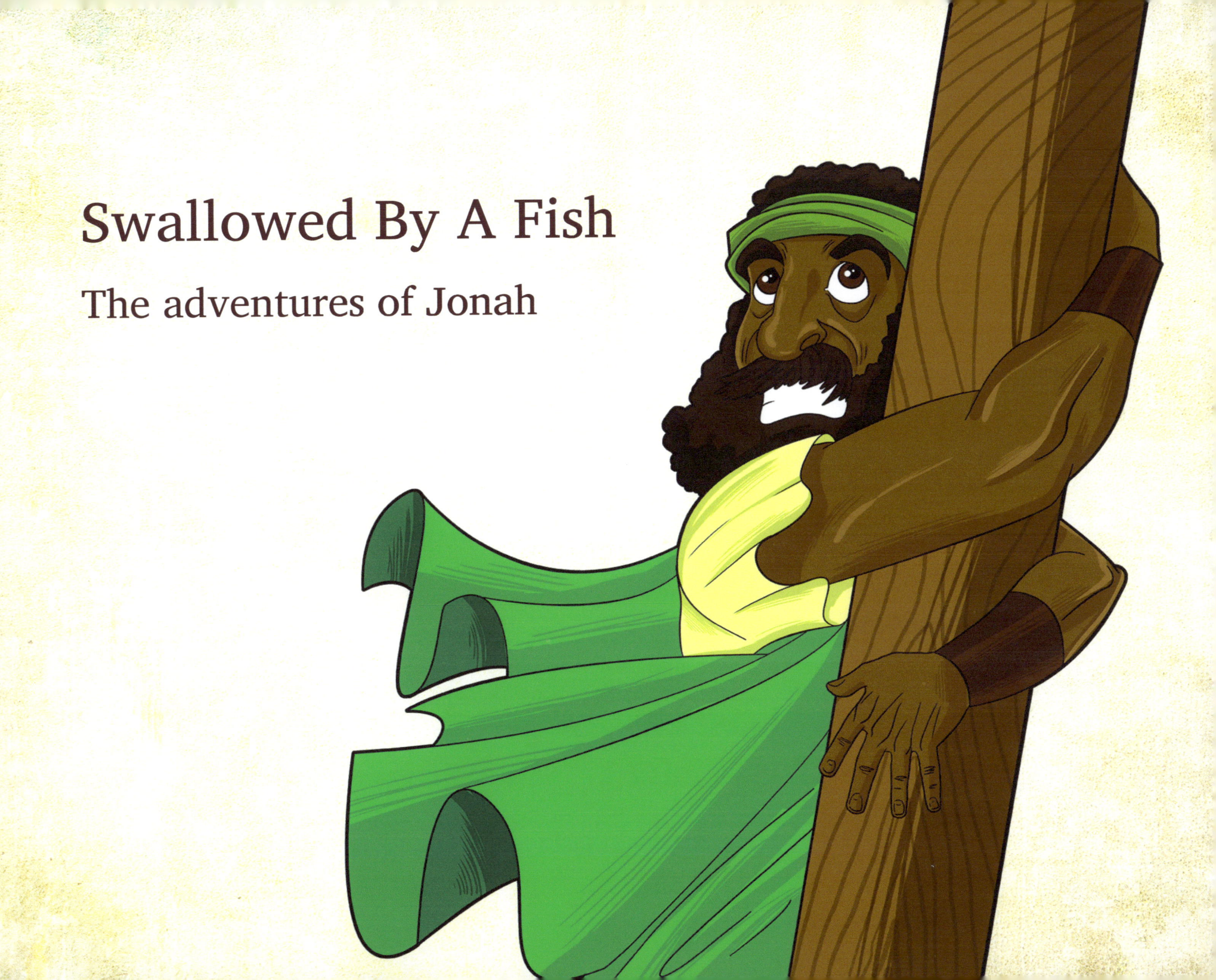

Swallowed By A Fish

The adventures of Jonah

"Now God had prepared a great fish to swallow up Jonah. And Jonah was in the belly of the fish three days and three nights." (Jonah 1:17)

Have you ever wondered what it would be like to be a prophet? What would it be like to give people messages from God? That was Jonah's job until Yahweh, the God of Abraham, Isaac and Jacob, sent him to give a special warning to a city of strangers.

Even worse, those strangers were his enemies! No wonder he didn't want to do the job God gave him.

Jonah was a Hebrew prophet who lived in the land of Israel a long time ago. God used him to deliver important messages to the Israelites. Sometimes these messages were warnings; other times, God gave Jonah good news to share.

You might think Jonah was very holy to be used by God, but he was just like us. He didn't always behave how God wanted him to behave.

Did you know?

Many people believe there are different ways to pronounce God's name. These include Yah, Yahweh, Yahuah, and many others.

During this time, King Jeroboam II ruled the land of Israel. He was a very rich and wicked king. He built huge palaces instead of helping the poor, and he worshipped false gods instead of worshipping God. Despite this, God still loved the people of Israel.

One day, God gave Jonah a message for the king. "Tell King Jeroboam that Israel will conquer its enemies. He will win back the land that was stolen, and Israel will become a mighty nation."

Jonah swallowed hard and stared at the ground. The thought of giving the king a message from God gave him goose bumps. What if it didn't come true? The king might throw him in jail for the rest of his life, or even worse, kill him!

The next morning, Jonah threw on his finest tunic and dashed through the busy streets to the royal palace. He marched up the steps and bowed before the king. "Your majesty, I have a message from God," said Jonah, clearing his throat.

"What is it?" snapped King Jeroboam. He scowled at Jonah from his large golden throne. He didn't like prophets with messages from God. They usually told him things he didn't want to hear. He tapped his fingers impatiently.

"Go and fight the Assyrians," Jonah told him. "God will give you victory over your enemies, and you'll become a powerful king." King Jeroboam smiled and puffed out his chest. He liked the idea of becoming a great king.

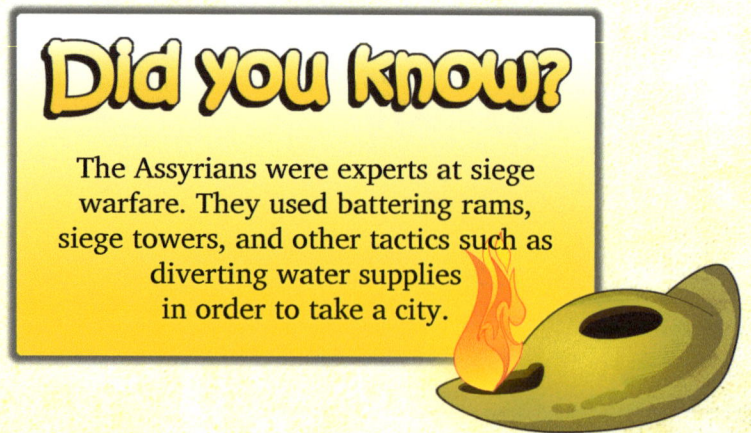

Did you know?

The Assyrians were experts at siege warfare. They used battering rams, siege towers, and other tactics such as diverting water supplies in order to take a city.

Later that week, the king gathered all his horses, chariots and soldiers and marched out to fight the powerful Assyrians. He captured the city of Damascus and won back the land that belonged to the people of Israel.

Jonah breathed a sigh of relief. Phew! God's message had come true. Being a prophet was much easier when God had good news to share. But God had another job planned for Jonah. One day, while Jonah prayed under an olive tree, God said to him, "Jonah, I want you to go to the city of Nineveh in Assyria."

Jonah frowned. He didn't like the sound of that idea at all. No one liked the Assyrians. They were as bloodthirsty as sharks! "If I go to Assyria, the Ninevites will kill me," said Jonah. He wiped the sweat from his brow. "Why would God send me there?"

God ignored Jonah's feeble protests. "Tell the Ninevites that they are a wicked people," He said. Jonah wasn't keen on telling the Ninevites anything. Why couldn't God just punish them for being wicked? He sat under the olive tree, staring grimly into the distance.

"What if the Ninevites repent?" Jonah asked God. He knew that God was a God of both judgment and mercy. "I could look like a fool, and Israel might not become a great nation!"

Jonah's thoughts and fears consumed him. He came up with a silly plan. He decided to ignore God's instructions and escape to a land far away.

That night, Jonah grabbed his satchel and fled to the city of Joppa. Joppa's harbor was full of ships, and Jonah knew he could find one that would take him far away from Nineveh. He made his way through the bustling crowds down to the busy port.

Jonah stood on the pier and watched the sailors load jars of oil and wine onto the ships. *I wonder if there's a boat leaving today*, he thought. At the end of the pier, he spotted a Phoenician ship bound for Tarshish. Tarshish was as far from Nineveh as he could get! He hurried over and introduced himself to the captain.

"Do you have space for one more?" asked Jonah. He pointing to the packed boat. The captain laughed greedily and nodded. "Ten silver coins," he said. He shot out a fat hand and waited for Jonah to count his money. Jonah paid for his ticket and scurried up the gangplank, his head bowed. He knew God was not pleased with this plan.

Did you know?

Many scholars believe Tarshish was located on the far side of the Mediterranean Sea, near Spain.

Soon, the sailors were ready to leave for Tarshish. Jonah was relieved—maybe he could get away from God after all! But God still knew what Jonah was up to. As the ship crept across the Mediterranean Sea, God sent a violent storm. Winds roared through the sails like a tornado, and waves pounded the sides of the ship.

"The boat will break into pieces and we'll drown," wailed the sailors over the howl of the wind and the waves. "What have we done to deserve this?" Every sailor cried to his own god to save them, but the seas grew higher and higher.

The captain stood in the middle of the ship, his arms wrapped tightly around the mast. "Throw some of the cargo overboard!" he shouted. "The ship will be easier to control." The sailors did as the captain commanded, but the boat still tossed about like a cork on the waves.

Meanwhile, the captain opened the wooden latch and peered into the dark hold. He couldn't believe his eyes! Jonah lay fast asleep, snoring like an elephant.

"Jonah, how can you sleep?" yelled the captain. "Get up and pray to your god. Maybe He'll feel sorry for us and save our lives."

Did you know?

Phoenician sailors were the world's most advanced traders at this time. They sailed across the Mediterranean, Atlantic, Red Sea, and Indian Ocean to trade with other nations.

Up on deck, the sailors were ready to start pointing fingers. They said to each other, "Let's draw straws and find out who's to blame for this storm." They drew Jonah's name and glared at him suspiciously.

"Why is this storm tormenting us?" they asked. "What are you doing here, anyway? Where are you from?"

"I'm a Hebrew," Jonah answered. "I serve God, the God of heaven. He created both the land and the sea." The sailors trembled with fear. They had heard all about the mighty God of the Hebrews.

"This horrible storm is all my fault," continued Jonah. He hung his head in shame. "If I had listened to God, we wouldn't be in this mess."

"Well, what can we do to stop the storm?" the sailors asked him. Jonah knew God was a just God, and would save the sailors lives. "If you toss me into the sea, the storm will disappear," he said.

The sailors liked Jonah. They didn't want to throw him overboard. Instead, they rowed harder and harder toward the shore. But the seas grew rougher, and the ship rowed round in circles.

Finally, the sailors cried out to God: "Please don't punish us for taking this man's life!" Grabbing Jonah by the arms and legs, they tossed him into the crashing waves. The sea instantly became as still as glass. The ship was saved!

God wasn't ready to let Jonah die. As the runaway prophet tumbled towards the bottom of the ocean, God sent an enormous fish to swallow him up. The fish liked this idea. It was hungry!

It opened its jaws as wide as possible, sucking Jonah into its enormous mouth. Jonah slid across its slimy pink tongue and nosedived into its dark, empty belly. It was steamy, sticky and black as midnight.

Jonah stood up and opened his eyes. He could not see even a single thing. His heart quaked with fear and he fell to his knees and wept.

Did you know?

A prophet is someone specially chosen by God to speak His truth. It can be hard to be a prophet, especially since prophets often say things people don't want to hear.

For three days and three nights, Jonah lived inside the enormous fish. It was the longest three days of his life! Jonah wished he had obeyed God. He prayed like he had never prayed before.

Finally, God told the fish to spit Jonah out of its dark steamy belly. The fish opened its mouth and sneezed.

Aaaachoo!

Jonah flew through the air like a spear and landed with a thump on the white, sandy beach. He was near enemy territory now, but he didn't care. He was ready to obey God. Jonah never wanted to live inside a fish again.

Jonah lay sprawled on the beach like a starfish, covered in fish slime and sand. He was finally ready to listen to God.

"Jonah, get up and go to the great city of Nineveh," said God. "Tell the people to repent."

Jonah jumped to his feet. He didn't want to be known as the smelly prophet. Racing down to the water's edge, he washed his tunic in the calm blue sea. Then, he threw on his leather sandals and set off for Nineveh as fast as his wobbly legs would carry him.

A few days later, Jonah arrived at the gates of Nineveh. He paused and stared at the thick brick walls that protected the city. A fearsome statue of the false god Lamassu stood guard, its stony eyes fixed on the people below.

Where do I start? wondered Jonah. He scratched his beard. The city walls stretched as far as the eye could see. He hadn't realized Nineveh was THIS big!

Jonah took a deep breath. He knew it was time to give the people God's message. He strode past the soldiers guarding the gate and made his way into the city. "In forty days, Nineveh will be overthrown!" shouted Jonah. He walked from one side of the city to the other. "Repent and turn to God's ways."

The Ninevites peered out of their houses and listened carefully. Much to Jonah's dismay, they believed God's message and wanted to stop their bad behavior. Tearing off their clothes, they put on sackcloth to show that they had repented.

Did you know?

At the time of Jonah's visit, Nineveh had a population of 100,000 people. It was protected by a large stone wall around the city so wide that two chariots could race on top of it, side by side!

When the King of Nineveh heard Jonah's message, he leapt from his throne, tore his fine robes and put on sackcloth. Then, he plonked himself down in a big pile of ashes. It might be hard to imagine a king getting so scared, but he had heard all about this mighty God of the Hebrews.

Later that day, the king rose to his feet and made an announcement. "No person or animal is to eat or drink anything," he said. "Everyone must wear sackcloth, pray to the God of the Hebrews and give up their wicked behavior."

The king turned to his officials. "Who knows? Maybe God will stop being angry and we won't die." The king was so serious about Nineveh's repentance that he even made the animals wear sackcloth! When God saw that the Ninevites had given up their evil ways, He decided not to punish them. The people of Nineveh were relieved!

Did you know?

Repentance means turning to God. The Bible says, "I preached that they should repent and turn to God and prove their repentance by their deeds."
(Acts 26:20)

Jonah was not happy. He wanted God to destroy Nineveh. If God let Israel's enemies live, the Israelites would never become a great nation! "God, didn't I say this would happen?" moaned Jonah. "I knew you'd forgive the Ninevites if they repented. Now people will think I'm a fool. Why don't you just let me die?"

"What right do you have to be angry?" replied God. Jonah didn't have an answer. He turned his back on Nineveh and marched out of the city gates to a hill overlooking the city. Using branches, he made himself a shelter and waited to see what would happen next. "Maybe God will change his mind and destroy Nineveh," said Jonah hopefully.

God decided to teach Jonah a lesson. He made a plant grow to protect Jonah from the blazing sun. Jonah stretched out in the shade and smiled. *This is more like it*, he thought. But at dawn the next day, a worm attacked the plant. Its leaves shrivelled up until there was nothing left. The sun beat down on Jonah's head until he nearly fainted.

"God, I can't stand this heat any longer," moaned Jonah. "It's hotter than a volcano. I'd be better off dead. Just let me die!"

"Do you have a right to be so angry about the plant?" asked God. "Yes, I have every right to be angry," said Jonah. "I'm angry enough to die!"

"The plant grew in one day and disappeared the next," said God. "You didn't make it grow, yet you're still upset it's gone! I made the people of Nineveh, from the old grandparents to the little children. Don't I have a right to be concerned about them? After all, the people don't know what they're doing."

Jonah bit his lip and stared at the dusty ground. He knew God was right. And from that day onwards he decided to never disobey God again.

THE END

TEST YOUR KNOWLEDGE!

(Match the question with the answer at the bottom of the page)

QUESTIONS

To which city did God tell Jonah to take His message? ....

Where did Jonah try to run to instead of going to Nineveh? ....

Where did Jonah board a ship? ....

What did Jonah do during the storm? ....

What did the sailors do to try and save the ship? ....

What happened after Jonah was thrown overboard? ....

How long was Jonah inside the belly of the fish? ....

Where did Jonah go after reaching dry land? ....

What did Jonah tell the people when he reached Nineveh? ....

What killed the plant that God provided Jonah for shade? ....

ANSWERS

1. Nineveh
2. Tarshish
3. Joppa
4. He slept
5. Threw the cargo overboard
6. Jonah was swallowed by a great fish
7. Three days and three nights
8. Nineveh
9. Repent
10. A worm

Complete the Word Search Puzzle

JONAH   PROPHET
JOPPA   FISH
NINEVEH CAPTAIN
WORM   SHIP
PLANT   REPENT

```
P F N I N E V E H R
F R V V O J H J N E
I C O W R T A P J P
S G A P V G R L O E
H S E P H W S A N N
R E Q C T E U N A T
E P Y U D A T T H R
S H I P A Q I D B A
R J O P P A C N G T
W O R M L T S H G L
```

Bible Pathway Adventures®

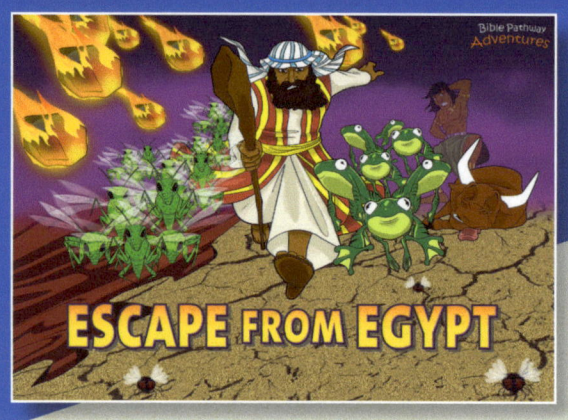

Facing the Giant
The Risen King
Saved by a Donkey
Thrown to the Lions
Witch of Endor
Sold into Slavery
The Great Flood
The Chosen Bride
Shipwrecked!
The Exodus
Escape from Egypt
Birth of the King
Betrayal of the King

Discover more Bible Pathway Adventures' Bible stories!

Check out Bible Pathway Adventures' Activity Books

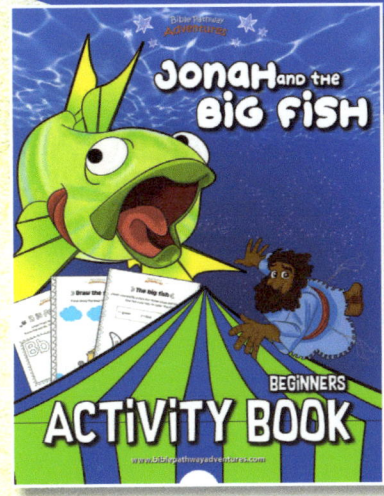 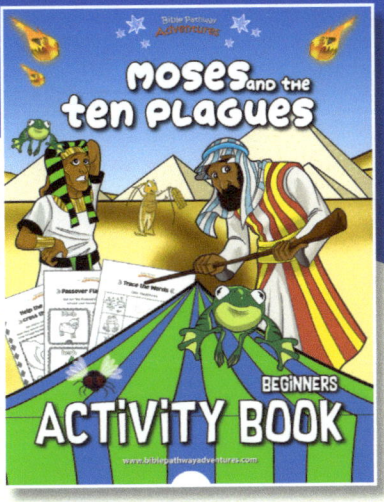 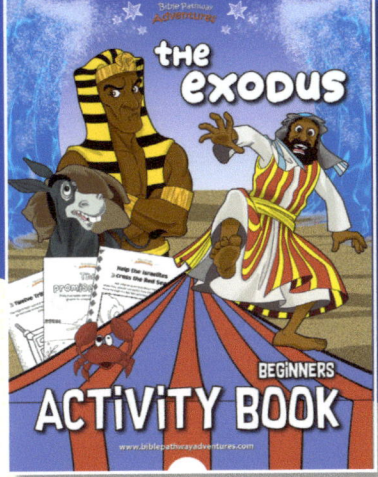 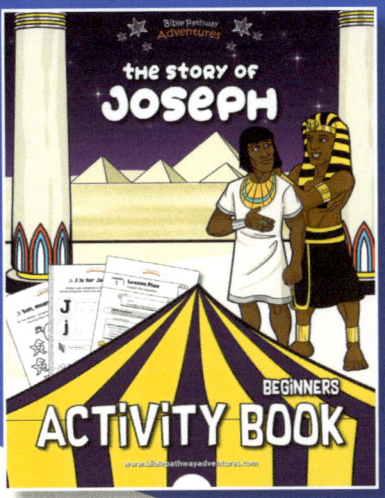

 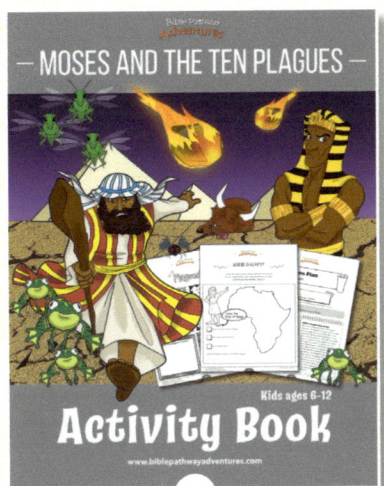 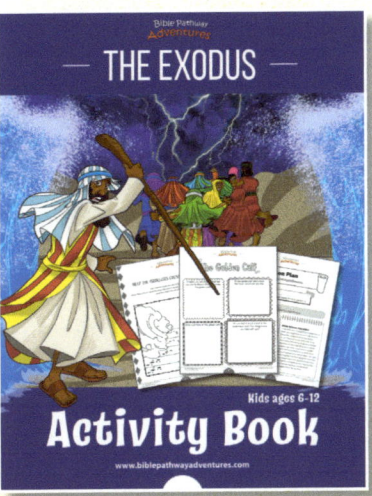 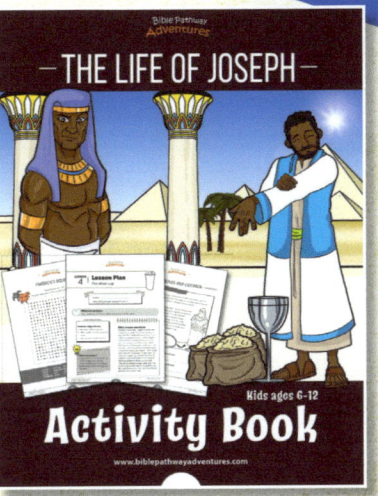

GO TO

www.biblepathwayadventures.com

www.ingramcontent.com/pod-product-compliance
Lightning Source LLC
Chambersburg PA
CBHW041323290426

44108CB00004B/116